CELEBRATE!
IN
SOUTH
ASIA

BY JOE VIESTI AND DIANE HALL
PHOTOGRAPHED BY JOE VIESTI

LOTHROP, LEE & SHEPARD BOOKS
NEW YORK

(ABOVE) Buddhists in Anuradhapura, Sri Lanka, gather at temples before dawn to offer incense and prayers on Wesak, believed to be the anniversary of the birth, enlightenment, and death of the founder of Buddhism.

(PREVIOUS PAGE) A young dancer celebrates Baishakhi (Bengali New Year) in Dhaka, Bangladesh.

Text copyright © 1996 by Joe Viesti and Diane Hall

Photographs copyright © 1996 by Joe Viesti

All rights reserved. No part of this book may be reproduced or utilized in any form or by any means, electronic or mechanical, including photocopying and recording, or by any information storage and retrieval system, without permission in writing from the Publisher. Inquiries should be addressed to Lothrop, Lee & Shepard Books, a division of William Morrow & Company, Inc., 1350 Avenue of the Americas, New York, New York 10019.

Printed in the United States of America

First Edition   1 2 3 4 5 6 7 8 9 10

Library of Congress Cataloging in Publication Data

Viesti, Joe F. Celebrate in South Asia / by Joe Viesti and Diane Hall.

p.   cm.   Summary: Describes religious festivals and sacred days celebrated in India, Sri Lanka, Bangladesh, Pakistan, Bhutan, Burma, and Nepal.

ISBN 0-688-13774-1. — ISBN 0-688-13775-X (lib. bdg.).

1. Festivals—South Asia—Juvenile literature. 2. South Asia— Religious life and customs—Juvenile literature.

[1. Festivals— South Asia. 2. Holidays—South Asia. 3. South Asia—Social life and customs.]

I. Hall, Diane. II. Title. GT4875.5.V54 1996 394.2'6954—dc20 96-6315 CIP AC

ust as we do in the United States, people in South Asia come together to celebrate holidays with song and dance, food and fun, parades and prayer. But the holidays and the ways in which they are celebrated often seem very different from our own. There are many reasons to celebrate—the beginning of the new year, the gathering of the harvest, to commemorate an important event, and to thank God—but whatever and wherever the celebration, it is always a time to forget about workday routines and appreciate the really important things in life: family, beliefs, and traditions. What better way to meet the people of the world than at a celebration!

A dancer reenacts a Bhutanese legend at the Paro Tsechu in Paro, Bhutan.

HOLI

Unlike most festivals in Asia, during Holi everyone wears his or her *worst* clothes. There are many versions of the origin of this ancient festival. On the day after the full moon in February or March, people take to the streets to throw *gulal,* a colored powder, at everyone within range. Adults usually rub the *gulal* onto one another's faces. Children gleefully squirt all comers with a mixture of *gulal* and water. By the end of the day, buildings, streets, and people are thick with splashes of red, pink, and purple paste that can take days to wash off. No wonder Holi is often called the "Festival of Color."

Holi falls at the end of the month of Phalguna (February or March), a time when everyone has spring fever. According to Hindu legend, even the god Krishna got caught up in the Holi merrymaking when he was growing up near Vrindavan, India, where these pictures were taken.

INDIA

PUSHKAR CAMEL FAIR

Pushkar, in the state of Rajasthan, India, is an important Hindu religious site. And for four days every November, it is also home to the world's largest camel fair. Since the fourth century, thousands of herders have gathered here to buy and sell camels and other livestock. The dunes outside of town are transformed into a sea of camels—nearly ten thousand of them. It is a spectacular sight. But as overwhelming as it is to the eye, it is even more overwhelming to the nose!

A Rajasthani herder shows off a prize camel.

There are camel games and races, too, including the thrilling camel rush: Teams of men jump on top of the sturdiest camels at the fair, and the camel that can hold the most men at once wins the contest.

At dawn during the Pushkar fair, a herder rouses his reluctant camel. He is wise to keep his distance. Camels are notoriously bad-tempered and may bite or spit at an unwary handler.

ESALA PERAHERA

A modern addition to the raja's costume is strings of electric lights run by battery packs.

Sri Lanka, the island republic off the southern coast of India, is the land of *peraheras* (processions). The most spectacular is the Esala Perahera in the city of Kandy. It lasts for ten days in July or August. The Esala Perahera is held in honor of a sacred relic—one of the Buddha's teeth—which has been protected in Kandy's Temple of the Tooth for more than two thousand years.

Thousands of dancers, drummers, and acrobats in traditional costumes participate in torchlight spectacles that build in excitement with each passing night. The climax comes on the last night, when more than one hundred elephants, glittering with silk, gold, and jewels in all the colors of the rainbow, slowly parade over a mile-long route under the full moon. Whip crackers clear the path, and torch spinners light the way for the elephants.

The senior elephant, called the "raja," heads the procession. On his back he carries a golden casket containing the sacred tooth. A crimson canopy is held above the raja, and a white cloth is spread before him. Legend has it that if you look closely, you may see a tear in the raja's eye because he is so proud to bear the Buddha's tooth.

Young boys carry offerings of flowers to pay homage to the relic of the Buddha's tooth.

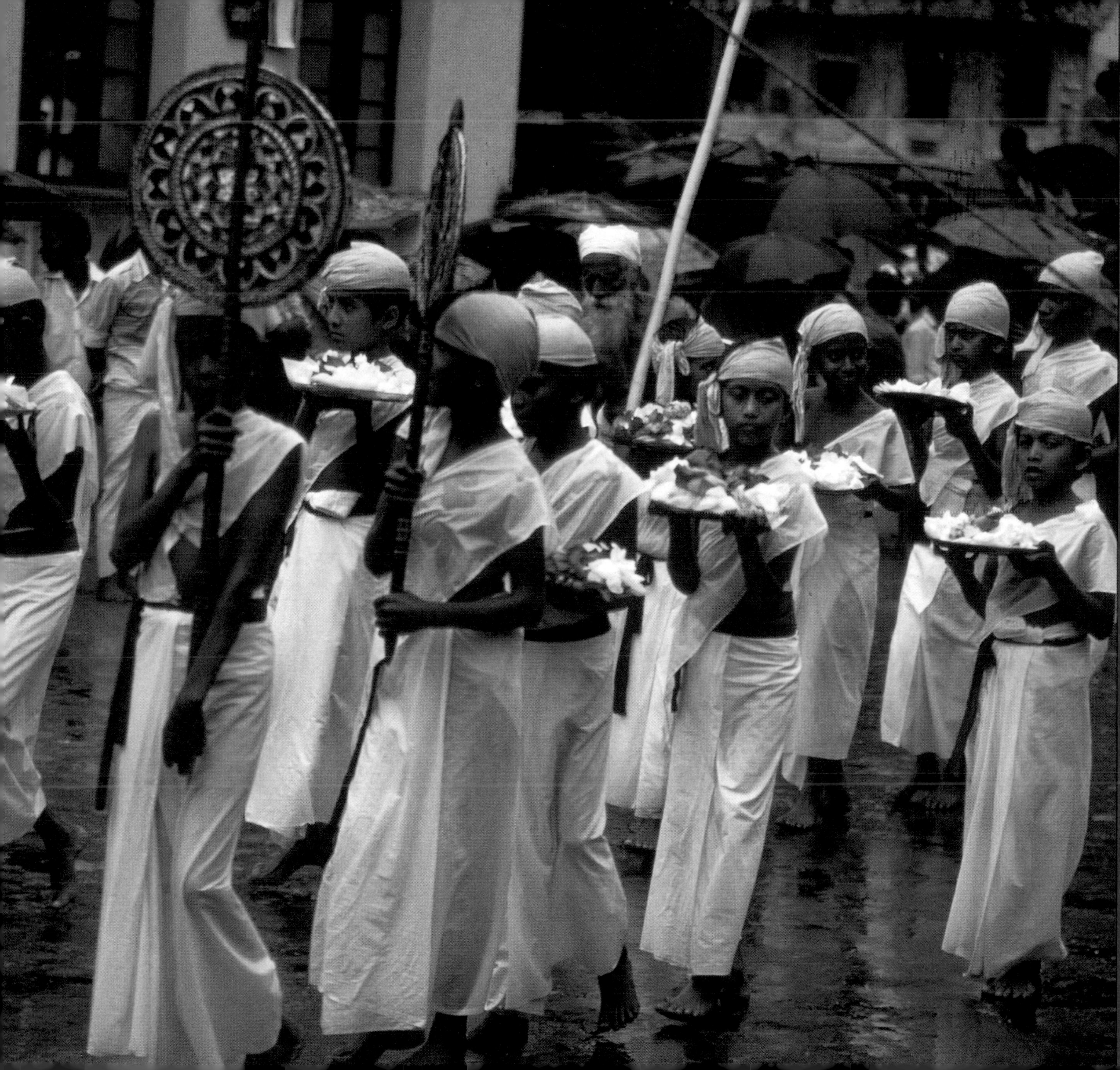

S R I L A N K A

The raja starts the *perahera* in daylight, but it is late at night before the hundreds of elephants and thousands of dancers, drummers, and performers finish the mile-long route.

SRI LANKA

WESAK

An elaborate *pandal* shows the enlightened Buddha.

The most sacred date in the Buddhist calendar is celebrated on the day of the full moon in the month of Wesak (May). Buddhists believe that the birth, enlightenment, and death of the Buddha all happened on this day.

Temples and homes are adorned with lights and paper lanterns, and the sweet scent of coconut oil lamps fills the night air. *Pandals,* huge paintings showing scenes from the life of the Buddha, are erected in cities and towns throughout India and Sri Lanka. Many older people dress all in white and spend the day in pagodas, meditating and praying. But the young mingle in the streets, while music and stories of the Buddha's life blare from countless loudspeakers.

In Anuradhapura, an ancient Sri Lankan city, the Wesak celebration begins before dawn. By early morning, temples are crowded with people praying and making offerings of incense. Monks in saffron-orange robes chant *sutras* (hymns to the Buddha) throughout the day, and worshipers give them gifts of food and money as a ritual act of charity. People flock to an ancient banyan tree that is believed to have grown from a cutting of the tree under which the Buddha reached enlightenment.

Many people dress in white during Wesak and gather together in meditation and prayer.

BAISHAKHI
(BENGALI NEW YEAR)

A Baishakhi *mela* food stall features piles of spicy fried snacks.

The Bengali New Year, called Baishakhi, is celebrated in April. It is a harvest festival, and farmers' children decorate their homes with colorful garlands of flowers. Farmhouse doorsteps are painted in traditional patterns to welcome new year's visitors, who are served rice cakes shaped like flowers. In towns, shopkeepers settle all their accounts from the old year, decorate their shops with flowers and streamers, and hand out sweets to children.

The highlight of the celebration is the Baishakhi *mela* (fair), with amusement-park rides and rows of stalls selling everything imaginable. In Dhaka, the capital of Bangladesh, the *mela* goes on for an entire week. At one minute past midnight on New Year's Day, Bengalis set off string after string of firecrackers. Later they greet the first sunrise of the new year with choral singing and poetry readings. On New Year's Day, people line the streets to watch the long procession of musicians and dancers perform.

This amusement ride at the Dhaka *mela* looks something like a Ferris wheel, but it is run by hand.

Bengali children preserve and celebrate their heritage by learning centuries-old songs and dances to perform during Baishakhi.

EID-UL-FITR

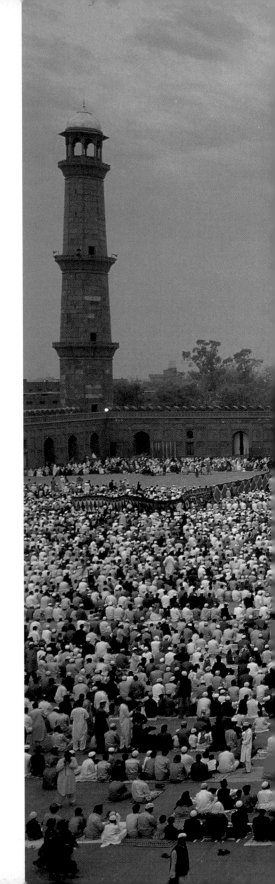

Eid-ul-Fitr means "breaking the fast." This Pakistani festival marks the end of Ramadan, the ninth month of the Muslim calendar, which usually falls in February or March. During the entire month of Ramadan, devout Muslims eat and drink nothing from sunrise to sunset.

Many Muslims buy new clothes to wear on Eid, and Pakistani shops and bazaars are crowded with customers. *Choorian*—colorful glass bangles—jingle on the arms of girls and women and are on sale everywhere you look. Children's shops are the most crowded. Pakistanis have a saying, "Eid is for children," and parents shower their sons and daughters with new clothes, shoes, and gifts of money called *Eidi*.

The first day of Eid begins early. After bathing, families get dressed in their new clothes and head to the mosque for prayers. Afterward, people exchange hugs and shout *"Eid mu-barak!"* ("Happy Eid!"). Then two days of feasting begin. Food sellers set up their stalls outside the mosques to serve hungry customers their first daytime meal in a month.

(RIGHT) The Badshahi Mosque in Lahore, Pakistan, can hold around 100,000 people. During Eid, so many come to pray that thousands must worship outside. (BELOW) *Choorian* sparkle in a Lahore shop.

PAKISTAN

PAKISTAN

(ABOVE) On the night before Eid, many Moslem girls and women decorate their hands and palms with intricate patterns drawn with a reddish-brown dye called henna.
(LEFT) After services, the people outside the Badshahi Mosque wish each other *"Eid mu-barak!"*—"Happy Eid!"

BHUTAN

PARO TSECHU

The kingdom of Bhutan is tucked high in the Himalaya Mountains between India and Tibet. Until 1964, the only way in or out of this tiny country was on foot or on horseback.

Every district of Bhutan has a castle monastery, called a *dzong*, which is the center of both government and religion. Throughout the year, Buddhist dance festivals, known as *tsechus*, are held outside in the courtyards of the *dzongs*. The dances reenact religious legends and famous events in Bhutanese history. The Bhutanese believe that a *tsechu* blesses and protects those who attend.

The best known of these festivals, the Paro Tsechu, takes place for six days in late March or early April. Hundreds of people travel for days on foot over rugged mountain paths to the Paro Valley. At dawn on the first day of the festival, a trumpet blasts from the *dzong* to announce the start of the *tsechu*, and the dances begin. The elaborate costumes and intricate dances have been passed down for hundreds of years. Many of the performers are monks, and for them dance is a form of meditation. But the *tsechus* are not only religious experiences. Between the sacred dances, *atsaras* (clowns) circulate through the crowd, families hold picnics, and groups of young people perform traditional folk songs and dances.

One of the sacred dances at the Paro Tsechu.

SHWEDAGON PAGODA FESTIVAL

In Myanmar (Burma), the full moon day in the month of Tabaung (February or March) is the time to celebrate pagodas. People visit their local pagodas to pray and leave offerings. They build sand pagodas to bring good luck.

In Rangoon (officially Yangon), Myanmar's capital, the biggest celebration is at the Shwedagon Pagoda. This ancient temple has endured for more than 2,500 years. It rises more than three hundred feet into the air, and its dome is covered with nearly two tons of gold, more than five thousand diamonds, and thousands of other precious jewels. Even from high above in an airplane, the Shwedagon glistens.

During the festival, the air is thick with the delicious aroma of deep-fried sticky rice, a popular Burmese snack. The steps leading into the pagoda are crowded with vendors selling tiny golden Buddhas, incense, and flowers to worshipers on their way to make offerings. Bamboo market stalls set up around the base of the pagoda display a dizzying array of handmade baskets, fabrics, pottery, and papier-mâché dolls from all over the country.

Buyers flock to a stall of flowers and incense outside the Shwedagon Pagoda.

MYANMAR

MYANMAR

(RIGHT AND ABOVE) This young boy is already destined to become a monk. Some Buddhist children enter monasteries at the age of three or four. (LEFT) Inside the temple, worshippers light candles and sticks of incense as they pray.

TiHAR
(NEWARI NEW YEAR)

epal, a Himalayan kingdom of breathtaking beauty, is a land of many festivals. Hardly a week goes by without some type of celebration, often more than one at a time!

Tihar is celebrated only by the Newari people of Nepal. This five-day long Hindu festival is associated with the dark, or waning, moon in October or November and also marks the Newari new year. It is a time of feasts and gift giving—more of a family celebration than a public one.

Each of the five days celebrates something different. The first day honors the sacred cow. Families decorate their cows with painted designs and wreaths of bright orange marigolds. A circle of mustard oil poured around a cow protects it from evil spirits. Dogs get the royal treatment on the second day of Tihar. Pets and strays alike are given mounds of special food decorated with *tika* (a colored paste made from dye and rice) and wear collars made of marigolds. The third day of Tihar celebrates Laxmi, the Hindu goddess of wealth and prosperity. Hindus believe that Laxmi will enter and bless only those homes where lights are burning to greet her. On this day every house, courtyard, roof, and garden is illuminated with lamps, candles, and electric bulbs. Young bulls are paid homage on the fourth day, and on the final day, sisters give thanks for their brothers.

This cow enjoys a tasty offering of grain on the first day of Tihar.

NEPAL

(ABOVE) TOP: **A woman strings a marigold necklace to adorn her cow.** BOTTOM: **This pet seems resigned to the worshipful attention it receives on the second day of Tihar.** (RIGHT) **A flute makes a good New Year's gift, so business is brisk for this vendor in Kathmandu during Tihar.**

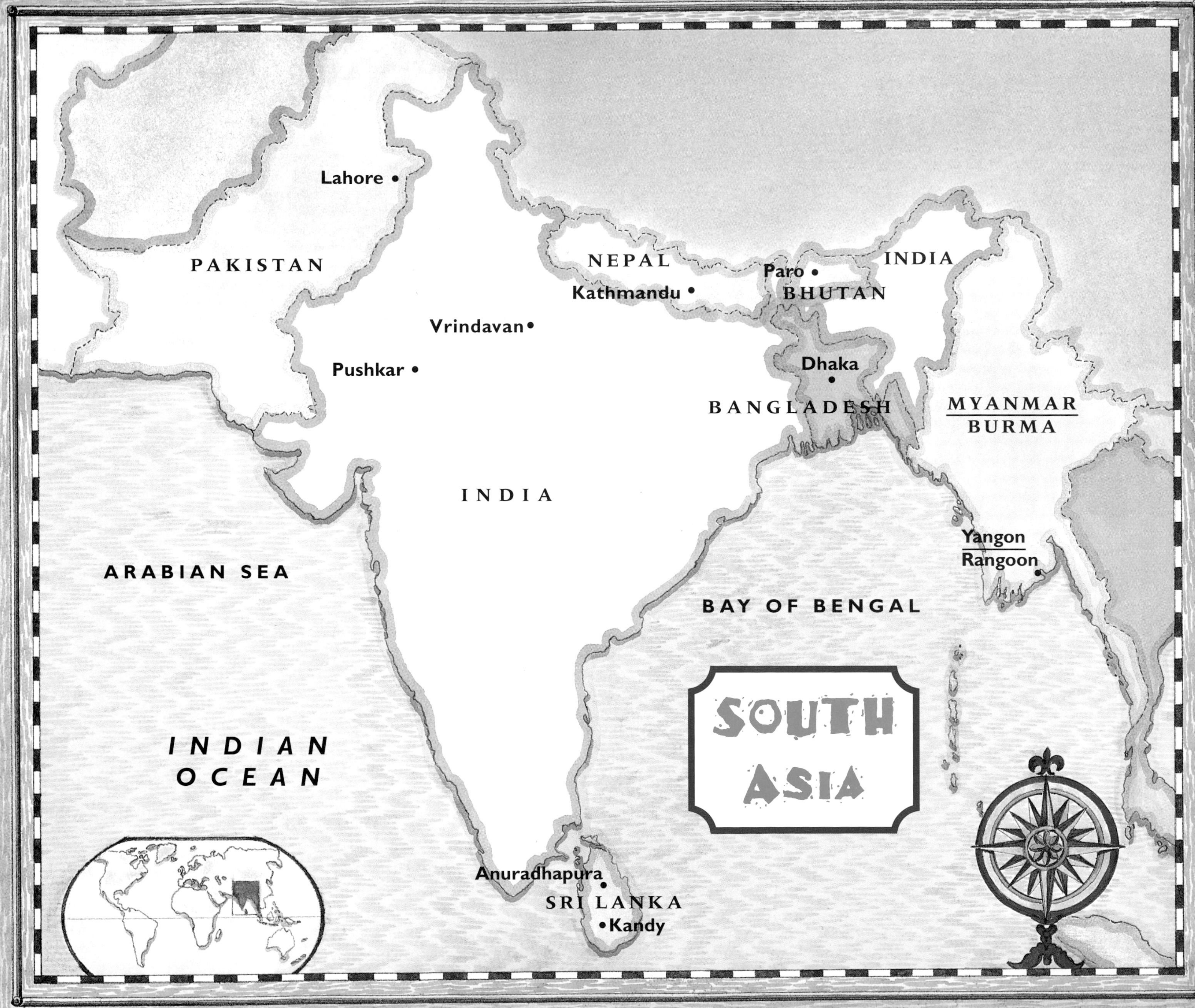

Lahore •

PAKISTAN

NEPAL

Paro •

INDIA

Kathmandu •

BHUTAN

Vrindavan •

Pushkar •

Dhaka
•

BANGLADESH

MYANMAR
BURMA

INDIA

Yangon
Rangoon
•

ARABIAN SEA

BAY OF BENGAL

INDIAN
OCEAN

SOUTH
ASIA

Anuradhapura
•

SRI LANKA

• Kandy